CW0034712A

A LIFE WORTH DYING FOR

Eben Britton
&
Augustus Britton

A LIFE WORTH DYING FOR

EBEN: Are you living a life worth dying for? Beautiful. What does this mean? 'A life worth dying for'. I have been thinking about it a lot. Are you living a life worth dying for? Are you willing to die for the life that you are living? How do you answer that question when you're totally identified in the mind, when you're totally identified and reliant on the intellect, when you totally believe in who you are on the outside? Your profession, religion, family, the position you hold in your community, are you willing to die for those things? Are you willing to die for the people that you love? That's *the* question in modern civilization. And it feels to me as though many people are walking around totally full of fear, willing to give up all semblance of themselves to *remain* comfortable. There's been a lot of bloodshed. There's been a lot of pain, a lot of suffering to get us to this point where we're unimaginably comfortable. A lot of people had to give up a lot of things to get us here. A lot of people were willing to die for the progression of humanity, for the progression of their loved ones, to keep people safe, to fight for what they believed in. And we are here today to figure out if humanity, in the year 2021, is willing to do that? And what does that mean?

AUGUSTUS: It's interesting to me because the way you are saying it feels like a more physical perspective. I was thinking of it in a *meta*physical perspective, in terms of whether or not you are living a life worth dying for.

EBEN: Well, that is a key of this whole question, because if you're wholly identified in the physical, you're probably not living a life worth dying for. You have to be rooted in some metaphysical truth or metaphysical reality to feel. To have the courage and the true strength it takes to die for the life that you're living.

AUGUSTUS: You said something important about not being able to feel, or being *able* to feel. I believe we're in a crisis of—particularly in America, but I assume this can spread out—I believe we're in a crisis of not feeling and a crisis of fear of death or a deep lack of acquaintance with death. Which, to me, so much of the pandemic, for instance, is about the impossible fact that we can't die. It's like we're clawing with our fingernails at the fountain of youth. But this is absurd, I recognize this absurdity from a Yoga perspective or a Buddhist perspective where impermanence is the game. Impermanence is basically the only game in town. In America we've completely lost that, we can't even talk about death in America, unless it's this sobbing trauma. Where it's 'Oh, no, we only reserve that for ridiculous action movies and funerals that happen, hopefully, once every 50 years or something'. You hit something important to me about not being able to feel. Which is why so many people don't meditate, because meditation gets you to the root of feeling, which I believe we can talk about later.

EBEN: I want to quote this gentleman named Zach Bush. I think this sums up the Western relationship with death. Bush is an MD, he's a triple board-certified physician. He applies the rigor of science, the strength of humanity and the intelligence of nature to transform our world. He has done two posts about death recently and it hits exactly what we're talking about.

AUGUSTUS: I had this incredible experience recently; can I tell it before you quote Bush?

EBEN: Yes. Go ahead.

AUGUSTUS: I went to the Post Office the other day, and as we know, Post Offices are like that movie Brazil; I don't know who got this job or what's going on or how these people are surviving. Papers everywhere. A mess. It's super rare to meet somebody at the Post Office who is nice. If they're nice or shed some peace and love they must be Buddha on the inside. Who knows what trip the nice Post Office clerk is on, cause that's a really interesting one. But anyway, I went to a Post Office and I was at the counter with a particularly ornery clerk. I asked her how she was doing and she didn't even look at me. Then this guy walks in without a mask on. Meanwhile, everyone else had a mask on because of COVID.

EBEN: Oh, wow. Where were you?

AUGUSTUS: Hollywood. The guy walks in without a mask on and I'm standing at the counter. And the clerk that wouldn't look at me, because she is clearly abjectly miserable, starts yelling at the guy without a mask on across the Post Office. 'Sir, put your mask on! Sir, you have *got* to put your mask on!' And he wasn't listening or paying attention. And then another Post Office clerk starts hollering at him. 'Sir! Put your mask on!' And I watched the display and I had a really interesting experience. I was like, 'what do you want him to put the mask on for?' A minute ago you looked almost dead. Dead inside. Emanating out. Like a coffin six feet underground sounded more interesting than this job you are doing. Suddenly some switch was flipped and you are totally meeting life, totally wanting and needing to hold onto life. You're miserable. What are you hanging onto? I think that's why it flashed to me to talk to you about this question of a life worth dying for. Which you brought up to me. When you told me that question or this ponderance it blew me away. The paradox and riddle of it blew my mind. *Is your life worth dying for?*

EBEN: If you are so encased in fear that you're not going out and living the life that you were destined to live, getting into adventures, risking the chance of inhaling some particle of some foreign body, which we're all doing all the time, anyway, which a mask is not doing anything to inhibit. And you're encased in this little tiny fear bubble, is that a life worth dying for? I would say 'no'. It's the interesting paradox of saying that you care about people's lives and you're so concerned with the sanctity of life yet you're not living! I love that Post Office story.

AUGUSTUS: Yes. If you're miserable then what are you holding onto? You're just clinging onto, what, some flicker of faith? Why not just go?

EBEN: Yeah. Good Lord.

AUGUSTUS: You probably believe in heaven. To a degree. Why not just go?

EBEN: Here's a quote from Zach Bush, *"We shouldn't fear the journey of death. It is our descent into our next birth canal. Something more beautiful than we can ever imagine, yet, as the inevitable approach of death becomes apparent all too often, our conventional medical system spends time flogging the failing body in an effort to beat back the dying process. Aggressive pharmaceuticals become a primary tool in nursing homes, hospitals, wards, and ICUs. They use antibiotics, steroids, ventilators, electroshock, cardiac resuscitation. As these fail in the last few weeks, we finally realize that the quality of life is more important than a fight for a longer life. We then move into hospice. As we approach our final days in our physical body, in the US healthcare system, the average hospice transition to death is only three weeks. Unfortunately, the fear does not relent in our behavior, even then in our pharmaceuticalized hospice practice, the dying process has increasingly become a pathway into narcotics. Benzodiazepine sedatives, anti-psychotic drugs, and a mess of symptom management medications to treat the side effects of those medications. This path is even more likely when hospice teams are not involved in such a hospice journey. The death transition is thoroughly blunted by the drug induced fog. The individual can be unable to communicate and experience the beauty of letting go of fear, lifelong doubts and insecurities. Therefore, they're unable to feel the expansion coming while still in their body. Unfortunately, not only are they missing out, but humanity is missing out being the witness to this* *journey, their children and grandchildren don't get to see the rebirth happen for all the perception of these paths. It really does smack an awful end point and we fear death as a result."*

AUGUSTUS: I love that.

EBEN: *"Our conventional medical system spends time flogging the failing body in an effort to beat back the dying process."* When did we decide that dying wasn't supposed to happen? Death is the flip side of the life coin.

AUGUSTUS: That made me think of Allan Watts when he's talking about the horrors of keeping people alive. Extended in the colorless corridors with radio activity through your veins.

EBEN: The thing is that when you're really living you die a thousand deaths all the time. But when you're heavily identified in your ego and your ego identity in your mind of who you are, then no death can happen. 'Oh, I'm Jimmy. I can't die. Cause then I'm not going to have this house and I'm not going to be able to play with my friends and I'm not going to be able to buy this and that. It's like you've identified your way out of the present moment of the life equation.

AUGUSTUS: We've weaponized death. As opposed to making it a beautiful, natural part of the process. What's strange to me about even saying this right now is that I'm in the prime of my life, so to speak. It's interesting for me to speak cavalierly, in a way, about the death process and how it's beautiful and whatnot. But then how else do we reprogram the death-fear if we're not going take the time to unpack the unbelievable amount of crap in the suitcase?

EBEN: What a shame to turn this thing that's going to happen to all of us into something so awful. We are all going to die. Every single thing on this planet lives and dies. And we've turned it into this thing that we're not allowed to do. That's ugly. That's horrible. That's painful. That's sickening.

AUGUSTUS: You would think it would be a relief. That's the beauty. We're off the hook. There's a reason Yogis and Buddhists treat reincarnation as a linchpin of their belief system.

EBEN: That's what psychedelics show you. Psychedelics bring you to the edge. Or, for that matter, anything really difficult or out of the ordinary material scheme. Breathwork. Meditation. You take a heavy dose of psilocybin or do an ayahuasca ceremony.

AUGUSTUS: I did hot Yoga last night. I felt close to death. I figured I was going to die. I felt a complete surrender laying there.

EBEN: You have to surrender in order to live. Let it all go. What a beautiful experience to have that release. To take all of your insecurities, all of your lifelong doubts, all of the stuff that you've been holding onto for so long in a moment and drop it. Then it all reveals itself to be completely meaningless because you are this thing that's just traveling through this journey called 'life'. The beautiful paradox of it is if we don't get acquainted with death, if we don't get intimate with death, then we can't live.

AUGUSTUS: That's why I think athletes, to a degree, particularly a sport like football or rugby, where you're risking it all physically, might have a better idea of understanding the death equation. You're more on the edge. In a way. Maybe. I just think when you're closer to that physical edge the better you will be. Feel pain. Bleed. A little bit. Know you're not a robot. Even just a little. Because everything is so mechanical. Get out of that system of thinking. Like in the hot Yoga class I thought I was done.

EBEN: There is that moment in the hot Yoga class where your body literally feels like it's going to combust. Your skin gets boilingly hot. Death is close, or at least the consideration is there, then life becomes precious like a diamond.

AUGUSTUS: Yogis carry around what's called a skull cup, which is the top half of a monk's skull. It's where they eat their food from. They turn all the food energy that people give them in their skull cup into divine energy and they eat it. They eat this stuff and it keeps them intimate with death. I bring that up because there's many different religions and places where death is cherished or at least it used to be cherished or *can* be cherished through their literature and methods. Do you feel like this is an America problem? A western problem?

EBEN: A western ideology? Yes. America, in particular, because we are the capital of materialism, almost our entire way of being is built on consumption and it's built on identity and all of our success paradigms are built on externalized concepts. People will convince themselves that they are nobody if they don't have the car and the job and the money and the house and the title. Who am if I don't have those things? What is my purpose? The materials are actually empty. *Are you willing to die for your BMW? Are you willing to die for the millions of dollars?* Maybe then you'll be willing to die for millions and millions of dollars. But then probably not. If someone came to your home and said, 'we're going to take you and your family prisoner, unless you do X, Y, and Z'. What are you going to do? Are you willing to fight? Are you willing to give it all up? And in this day and age in America, we love to say, 'Oh, that'll never happen. No one's coming to do that. No one will come and try to take things from me'. Oh, really? It's happened throughout history. Just because we live in this country called America in 2021. This golden age of excess. That means nothing. That's completely meaningless in terms of how fragile it is.

AUGUSTUS: It's as if our culture is built on the shoulders of golf tees.

EBEN: All of it is a total illusion. 'You're entitled to your comfort, but only if you do X, Y, and Z'.

AUGUSTUS: I'm currently reading this book called *It's Here Now, Are You?* It's by Bhagvan Das, he was Ram Dass' guru brother, he introduced Ram Dass to their guru Neem Karoli Baba. I thought this passage from the book is apt to tell. The passage is about when Bhagavan lived on and around these cremation grounds in India and meditated on Kali Ma, who is the goddess of death and rebirth, and he speaks about shakti, which is energy, essentially. Bhagavan says, and this is a memoir, keep in mind, *"There was so much Shakti. Kali Ma was everywhere, but the cremation grounds were her favorite haunt. There were lots of bodies lying around but no people—just demons. I needed the reality of death in my life because death reminds me to go to God. I vowed to stay there for two weeks.*

It was the longest two weeks of my life. After the first day, I saw enough death to last a lifetime—at least four or five bodies during the first hour. And the bodies all came with funeral parties. Everyone was moaning and grieving and miserable.

"Ram nam satyahai satyabol sattyahai!" ("God's name is true, say the truth, it is true.") They chanted as they brought the bodies down on bamboo poles with cloth stretched across. Business was brisk. In those two weeks I must have seen over fifty bodies, a steady stream coming in every day, and I saw the whole drama—the depth of people's attachments and loss.

After being there for three days, I was incredibly alert. Wide awake. There were fifteen funeral pyres on one side of the road and 12 pits dug in the ground on the other side. Outside the cemetery wall at the very back was the baby graveyard—tiny skulls everywhere. They didn't burn infant corpses in India, they just threw them over the walls to be devoured by jackals and wild hyenas.

Howling dogs were always around, which added immensely to the atmosphere. They'd fight over a rib cage and tear arms and legs to pieces. I thought, life is not a test. Life is the real thing. And there's nothing in life more real than death."

EBEN: Holy cow. That would make 90 percent of Americans quiver in horror.

AUGUSTUS: What about the people that would say to us, 'how undignified of you. How grotesque and unsanctified of you guys to think you can just throw death around. People are dying, man'.

EBEN: No shit. People have always been dying. What, do you think that's new and that just started this year? People just started dying?

AUGUSTUS: How does one get to living a life worth dying for? What has your process been?

EBEN: Walking through the fire. Shedding the skins. Getting down to the core essence. Living from my heart. What do I love to do? Filling my days with what I love to do: creating art, being out in nature, moving my body, breathing deeply, meditating, spending time with my loved ones. Being able to move about this planet at free will, at my simplest desire. I wasn't willing to die when I played pro football, I wasn't willing to die for that life. I used to think about this thought back then.

AUGUSTUS: Our mother always would say to you before games, 'It's a good day to die'.

EBEN: Yes. She always said that. It's a Native American saying. They say it's from the Lakota war leader Crazy Horse, but allegedly it was first attributed to Lakota chief Low Dog. Mom would say that to me before every football game. And for a long time I loved that. And I believed in it, and I always felt it on game day, but there came a point in my football career where I was like, 'I'm not willing to die for this'. I'm willing to die for the life I live right now, though. *Today.* Yeah. If someone or some army came marching through the streets of Los Angeles and started telling people what you had to do to continue your way of life or else you're going to be killed. All right, brother, we're going to battle to the death. Cause that's where I'm at in my life right now. The way I live is worth dying for. Breathing deeply. Being able to walk into the mountains whenever I feel so inclined. Meditating. Creating my art, spreading this message. But my life is a constant shedding of the skin. The identities, all the bullshit. Superficial identities that get thrown over our lives. Those things are meaningless. That's not what I'm dying for. And when the army does march through the streets, whether it be spiritually or actually, the superficiality is not going to do you any good in the battle for your soul. No.

AUGUSTUS: Your sadhana (your practice to become your ultimate expression in this reality) is similar to my practice. Body movement, meditation, breath, fasting, shedding the skins through community and reading and writing.

EBEN: And sure you can make money and have a job too. If that's what calls to you. I couldn't work at a desk if I tried.

AUGUSTUS: And know your zip code. That's a good idea, I guess.

EBEN: I couldn't work for someone else. I've tried it. It doesn't work. My soul is screaming to get out. And then I become negative. And when I'm negative. Woo! I infect an entire building. I'll set an entire building on fire with anger and resentment and rage. I did it. I've done it. I created a CBD company and I started coming into that building every day angry and pissed off. I watched it ripple out into other people. I'm like, 'what am I doing here?' I'm destroying this company through my energy. It's not worth it.

AUGUSTUS: You were dying there?

EBEN: Absolutely. I was miserable. I was dying. If you're miserable are you living a life worth dying for? That woman clerk at the post office.

AUGUSTUS: Just quit your job.

EBEN: Yes. Nobody's making you do it. A couple of weeks ago on a Tuesday afternoon I felt like crap. I had two weeks of feeling really tired, really overwhelmed, not feeling as inspired as I wanted to be. And it all culminated in this Tuesday afternoon. I'm sitting there and I'm thinking to myself, I'm just spinning my tires. I'm not making enough money. I'm not making *any* money, actually. I ask, 'does any of this matter?' 'Am I doing anything real?' 'Does anyone care?' 'What am I doing here?' I'm exhausted. Who am I kidding? What am I doing? I get the dogs on their leashes and my daughter and I take them for a walk around the block. And I've got all of this running through my head. The pity party. The shame spiral is coming in hot. I'm circling the drain. And all of a sudden this voice comes in and it goes, 'Is it about money?' And before I could answer, it says, 'go get a job. You can get a job right now, today. That'll start making you money. Is it about the money? Go get a job.' I thought to myself 'no, it's not about that.' Then it says, 'do you have faith in what you're doing?' I said to myself, 'yeah, I have total faith in what I'm doing. And I know that I'm exactly where I need to be.' And the voice said, 'then you're just playing a game with yourself of the little artist up against the world. Trust the process.' I looked up into the sky and the clouds parted and the sun beamed through and I was like, that's it. What do you want in life? Stop living the life that you think you're supposed to live. *Because living someone else's life is not the life that's worth dying for.* If you're living your life for somebody else because you think it's what you should be doing or what the society wants you to be doing, or what somebody told you, it's never going to work. You're never going to be rooted into your heart, into your truth, ready to die for what you believe in. I'm telling you this country would not be here without death. If there weren't thousands of people who were willing to die for what they believed in, for the ground they were standing on. Nothing.

AUGUSTUS: I've heard Allan Watts' main response when he would speak to college students or anybody for that matter, when they asked 'what do I do?' He said 'do what you would do if money didn't matter.' Do what you would do if money was not part of the equation. It's interesting. You bring up money. Money is a chokehold to living in this fantasy, this drama, as you're saying. You were playing out the drama of money, in a way. But if you're not choked by the money paradigm then you can feel the ground, you can see the truth. Which is why I believe meditation is important, because when we're committed to the material, when you're committed to the external and identification with 'I'm this and I'm that and I must live this way, et cetera.' Then living is just another word or impossible concept of future tripping, in the same way dying is. But when we meditate and we're silent and we get down to the core, our heart, our hridayam (our heart space), then it's all just true. I sense that people don't want to meditate or have an aversion to meditating because then you have to feel. And then there's just rain. There's just a waterfall. There's a Buddhist feeling akin to a waterfall of the mind. Once you sit there in meditation that waterfall comes and you feel all of the things. And it's really easy to convince yourself out of that situation, out of the silence, because you get on that train of external and material movement. 'Oh, man, that person's attractive. Oh, man, I need that shirt at the thrift store. Oh, man, I gotta go get a coffee now. Oh, It's dinner. Oh, man, is the date going to work out?' And before you know it you haven't meditated in 20 years. You haven't felt the truth for 20 years.

EBEN: All the money in the world can't buy you fulfillment. All the exterior play of material and fetishizing objects, that is what fills you with the sense of what life really is? Maybe for a little bit. But as long as you're just walking around the truth and filling your life with the meaningless materialist bullshit; the cars and the externals, and whatever thing you think is success and the expectations and the clothes, none of that ever does anything for you. But when you surrender to the experience of being a human of being in this body. Which I still am amazed by. I mean blown away. Sitting here right now, looking out of these eyes, talking with my mouth, making these noises, feeling all of this energy inside of me, the waterfall of experience. It's so much more whole than any material could offer me. It's unbelievably rich. And you're really made whole through the pain and through the discomfort and through the beauty and through all of it. It's so real.

AUGUSTUS: I may be broke in money but I'm rich in love. And I'm only getting richer. That's what's beautiful. The more you do the practice you're just getting more and more rich. I'm not saying there isn't hardship. I was in a hellscape of rejection three days ago.

EBEN: The world is insane. But how do you embrace it? What are you going to do? There's nothing to latch onto that's going to fulfill your expectations of it. If you're waiting for someone else to fill your expectations and make you happy and give you contentment you're screwed.

AUGUSTUS: I love this thing that you say. I've had an interesting journey with it. You would tell people to meditate for five minutes a day. And I had done TM (Transcendental Meditation), which is 20 minutes a day, twice a day, right. Maharishi Mahesh, who founded TM, would say, 'do 20 minutes twice a day'. And then I read different books where, you know, Jack Kornfield, for instance, would talk about being a monk and meditating for 18 hours a day. But then I would always hear you. And you came through with telling people to meditate for five minutes! And I always thought it was sort of silly. Like, five minutes, that's it? Come on, dude, give them *at least* 20. And you would be like just do five minutes. But that all changed for me the deeper I got into my meditating and the deeper I thought about the person that has never meditated before. And my God, I thought, if you can just give yourself five minutes. Five minutes of silence, that's more than enough, but five minutes can be mind-blowing. Let it build and grow into more time and more meditation, but for someone that has never meditated before, particularly in such a chaotically fast culture, five minutes can shift the world.

EBEN: It's beautiful. And it gives you that taste. Yeah. You get the taste.

AUGUSTUS: Ooh, wow. I was thinking of that the other day, get the taste, actually. Yes.

EBEN: All you need is a taste. I did this podcast yesterday and we talked a lot about psychedelics and how important psychedelics are for the Western culture, because people are adverse to the idea of sitting and meditating and the process of that unfoldment that it's like, we *need* psychedelics to blast us through, to open the door, to show us what we can be, what we *are*. And I really appreciated that sentiment. And I think that's very true and that's why psylocibin and ayahuasca, and 5-MeO-DMT, and cannabis, and all of these things are coming into the fold in America. Because we're in dire need. *We* *are in a spiritual and emotional crisis here in the Western world.*

AUGUSTUS: Absolutely.

EBEN: But I would say that the five minutes of meditation is key because it gives you that taste and you touch down. You're just like a feather. You touched down at the very bottom of yourself for a moment and you go, 'Whoa, I want more of that'. If you try to tell somebody who's never meditated before to go meditate for 20 minutes, they're going to be popping their eyes open every three seconds, looking at the clock wondering when it's over. That doesn't do us any good. People need to feel it. Rest into it.

AUGUSTUS: Yeah. Five minutes. You can feel it. Three minutes. You can feel it. Oh yeah. I've turned the timer off. To let go of the time paradigm.

EBEN: Now that's when you're really flowing, I feel you. Allowing the flow.

AUGUSTUS: But, as you say, and as I have said and felt for some time, it is not an accident that the psychedelic drugs are prominent now. They've been prominent since the sixties or so, but now they're becoming almost, I don't know, mainstream, it's no accident that cannabis is mainstream now.

EBEN: No, that's not an accident.

AUGUSTUS: We've needed this in this epoch. We're in dire need. It's a wakeup call. What are you? Are you living a life worth dying for? Are you really? Are the video games on the couch worth dying for? Are the Hot Cheeto covered chicken wings worth dying for? Boy, because those chickens died for you. I like to earn my meal, man. I like to earn my meal every day. What do you think of that?

EBEN: I love that.

AUGUSTUS: I like to earn this life. Whether I meditated or I went for a run. Earn that meal, brothers and sisters.

EBEN: Oh, yeah. I fast almost every single day. I know. I feel the food. I can't eat if I'm taking it for granted.

AUGUSTUS: I see that. There's light pouring out of your eyes. Meditating for five minutes. Close your eyes. Just get a taste. Feel the depth of your being. God. It's gorgeous. When you start to let go and just completely find yourself. How does a person do that if the veil is really thick? I'm thinking about the person that is in their veil that they can't even hear us right now.

EBEN: I think it's less about the thickness of the veil. In America, we have *so many* veils. Layers and layers of veils, right? It's not just one that we need to move through. Life is painful. Life is really difficult and challenging. That's the utter truth. And the sooner you are willing to embrace that death is real the better. Death is the flip side of the life coin. Yin and Yang, darkness and light, ebb and flow, the trough and the crest of the wave. It's all one thing. The sooner you are willing to open and embrace the fact that life is difficult and challenging you will begin to experience more joy. The door to joy and happiness will be open to you and be available to you, but until then you'll live a life of mediocrity and misery.

AUGUSTUS: And until then you will continue to not take responsibility.

EBEN: We're stepping into a new age because consciousness is moving very quickly. It's moving fast and evolving fast. Right now we can no longer afford unconscious living. And life and nature and the Universe are not going to be very kind to the unconscious people. These 'intellectuals' who base their belief systems on false paradigms are going to have to make a deep amends to the world for the wreckage they've caused very soon. It might not be in our lifetime, but the amends will happen.

AUGUSTUS: The Universe is not going to be kind to the unconscious karma. It's the weight. It's energy. You can't escape it. There's no outrunning karma.

EBEN: See the farmer now or the doctor later. Get out of the ignorance.

AUGUSTUS: Take responsibility. Take accountability. Be here.

EBEN: Whatever you want to call it. I don't care if you believe in God. If you believe in karma. These are just labels to describe the energy of the Universe that we inhabit. We've created this idea that we are separate from everything. *Ha!* We just spawned out of this thing. Just like everything else. Just like the tree came out of the earth. We came out of the Universe. We're a physical manifestation of the universal intelligence here.

AUGUSTUS: Oh, we're not separate at all. That helped me a lot, dropping the duality. This is a non-dual existence for me.

EBEN: How much time are you going to spend fighting against nature? Resisting nature. Spend all the time you want, spend all the energy you want, at the end of the day you're going back into it. *It. Nature.*

AUGUSTUS: I was trying to say something about us, the two of us, because we weren't always here, in this state of mind or state of heart, with these beliefs and convictions. That's why I brought up the veils. Because somebody is reading this and not even able to hear it, but I would say to that person, 'let us break the veil a little bit'. You don't even need to take it in. You don't even need to digest it. This could be just your taste. I love that idea of tasting it. Once you taste it it's hard to not want more. Once you get the taste of God or the taste of life, let's say, because some people aren't really interested in the word God, let's just say God is life. So now you get the taste of life. Where do you stop? *Where do you stop?* It's infinite. It's completely insane and incredible. You're just here in the now and the practice of deepening who you are becomes infinite because it *is* infinite.

EBEN: This is enough just being here now. This is beautiful enough. But God is also death.

AUGUSTUS: God is life and death. Yeah. It's hilarious. I was having a strange time with that. When our dogs died recently I wasn't crying. I know you had major sobs. But I wasn't crying. I was equanimous in a way. I felt like it was natural, the deaths. Maybe that's because I was listening to so much Ram Dass and him almost beautifying death, in a way. But I thought, what am I supposed to feel here? Through the American paradigm? Am I supposed to sob and break down and head for the hills, or am I supposed to honor this and understand that this is beautiful? Which, I think is what we came around to with your dog. Your dog's death became God. He's the great teacher. And his death was a great teacher.

EBEN: I think about my dog every day. Sunny is his name. I think Sunny is my guru in many ways. Pissing on things. Happy as a creature could possibly be. A beam of light. In India they celebrate death. The River Ganges. They send burning bodies floating down the river all day.

AUGUSTUS: Yeah. Bhagavan Das talks about that in his book. He would go swimming in the Ganges and bodies would float by him.

EBEN: They celebrate death as if it's a part of life because it is. It's life and death intermingling. Look at what we do to old people in America.

AUGUSTUS: You can't even see them. You don't even know where old people are in America half the time. They go to 'homes'.

EBEN: And now we have this weird thing in the COVID paradigm of 'protect the elderly'. What is that? We've been protecting the elderly? I don't think so. We've been shunning them and shaming them into darkness. Stay away from us. We don't want to see what happens when our dicks don't work and we need help shitting and our minds are breaking down and we're falling apart. Stay away. Give me a break.

AUGUSTUS: I love Ram Dass' perspective on old age and death.

EBEN: I recently heard him talk about going and hanging out with guys on death row. And he said it was like being in a temple of monks.

AUGUSTUS: That talk is beautiful.

EBEN: He said 9 out of 10 of the guys are totally surrendered to God. Pictures of Jesus and Gandhi and saints in their prison cells. Maybe a picture of a swimsuit model for laughs. And they're in their prison cells as deep as monks or Yogis or lamas, centered in the truth. I'm not saying you have to be on death row, but it is an interesting look, maybe, at what is possible. You might think if you were on death row you would melt down frantically, but it's actually a deep quieting down.

AUGUSTUS: I heard that Ram Dass talked to Elisabeth Kübler-Ross, who was a pioneer in the study of death and the near-death experience, and he told her about the death row inmate experience he had. He asked her what the deal was, something like 'why are we so out of touch with death?' And she said, 'don't you understand? *We are all on death row*'.

EBEN: Ah, so how do you live now?

AUGUSTUS: What are you going to do with this time?

EBEN: This intellectual paradox in terms of the reincarnation process is funny because people might go, 'well, if you reincarnate then it doesn't really matter what you do here in this lifetime'.

AUGUSTUS: Yeah, but you're trying to get free. In this one. Not the next one.

EBEN: And it may take you thousands of lifetimes to transcend, to get to that place of total liberation.

AUGUSTUS: Tell the silk scarf story.

EBEN: A student said, 'Hey Buddha, how long does it take to get enlightened?' What am I doing here? How many lifetimes is this? Can I do it in this lifetime? Buddha said, 'take a mountain—six miles wide, six miles deep, six miles tall. And every hundred years a stork flies over the top of the mountain with a silk scarf in its mouth and drags the silk scarf across the top. And the amount of time that it would take to wear down the mountain to nothing with the silk scarf is the amount of time it takes for you to be enlightened, or the amount of time you've spent in various incarnations'. Coming into life, out of life, into life, out of life. But, to me, when you really slow down and live in the moment and you live with pure presence and you're here—now you live a thousand lifetimes in a minute.

AUGUSTUS: Exactly. It's beautiful. Try it, ladies and gentlemen.

EBEN: Put down the phone. Amazing. Blow up your TV. Read a book. Step outside. Move your body. Take a deep breath and feel the magnificence of your humanness and your beingness. The profundity of this transcends all walks of life, all ways of being, because when you slow it down to zero, you are now blessed with the ability to do and create whatever thing you want. Out of nothing comes everything. Think about how fast you're moving right now, where your mind is; you've got a million emails to respond to, phone calls to make, meetings to schedule, people to talk to, to write tasks, to get errands done. Think about how overwhelmed you are with all of that right now. The thought of coming to zero to getting completely still, doing nothing, do absolutely nothing but breathe and sit there. It fills you with panic because you think that you're running out of time, but when you actually slow down to zero, bring it all the way down to nothing. All of a sudden you're blessed with the energy to do everything and anything you could possibly imagine and dream of. All of it gets done in a moment. Every email gets sent. Boom. Done. Without even a thought. It just happens because you've completely surrendered and let go.

AUGUSTUS: It's a beautiful practice to do for a week. To try. Experiment with. Just do nothing. Just see, just drop it, allow yourself to do nothing. Even that spirit form: I don't need to do anything. It's not to say just sit there, but to disidentify with thinking you're obligated to live some sort of acculturated life.

EBEN: Are you waiting for someone else to tell you what to do? That's the whole game. Are you waiting for the government to tell you it's safe? Are you waiting for the corporate news media to let you know that you can leave your house? Because if it's up to them you're toast, they've completely sold you out long ago. If you're waiting for them to tell you when it's safe to return to life, buckle up, because they're going to strap you in for a long ride.

AUGUSTUS: It's like the Samuel Beckett play *Waiting For Godot*. Godot never shows up.

EBEN: If they could get away with it we'd already be in the matrix. A feeding tube plunged down our throat and a tube up our ass pumping the shit out. Feeding the machines. Hey, man, if they could get away with it, we'd already be there.

AUGUSTUS: Who is 'they'?

EBEN: The Ego. The voice outside of you. The blinding of the still small voice inside you. I could say *'they'* are the corporations, which is what 'they' are, but 'they' is also the force blinding you from seeing the truth in your heart.

AUGUSTUS: And then there'd be a select few who are allowed to enjoy the fruits of nature, but that just doesn't work. Thankfully that doesn't work. There's too many people that are spiritually sane.

EBEN: What does a life worth dying for look like to you? That's what we should be creating and cultivating, our life as something that we are willing to die for. It should be so good, so rich, so delicious in its wholeness and its beauty that you are literally willing to lay down your life for all of it. Forget the whole 'I'll take what I can get, give me my little food pellet and my reality TV. Give me my little conveniences that make me comfy'. No thanks. And you know what? Once you come around to that realization, once you start having the feeling that, 'Oh, wow, I would die for this life'. You've eclipsed the old self. All of the apathy is not there anymore.

AUGUSTUS: You're going to be so full that it's almost like these concepts won't even exist anymore in your paradigm.

EBEN: Your life should transcend all methods, all concepts. It should not be about the Gucci belt, the BMW, the house, the car. Your life is not about that. Your life is not a brand. Your life is not a label. You are the Universe and nature in manifestation in motion. And you should honor the blessing of it; to experience all of it.

AUGUSTUS: Square one: open up and get quiet. Bring it down to zero. Square one: pull it back. Rebuild. Crumble. Tear the castle down. Let's see what the landscape looks like. When I was first moving into recovery someone said to me, 'now we get to look at the landscape of our unmanageability'. That was cool. I'm on this mountaintop. I'm looking at all the burning wreckage in the distance. Now let's create this new and beautiful landscape.

EBEN: I love that.

AUGUSTUS: But that doesn't happen unless we get down to square one, out of the denial that this isn't working anymore. The Gucci belt is not serving me anymore. The Gucci can't cover up the fact that you're a fallible human being who makes mistakes, who has experienced pain and trauma and who is living in a state of suffering. You can't buy away your pain.

EBEN: Nope. For a moment, maybe. It'll give you that little dopamine hit. A little 'ooh, wow. Look at this. Look at this new little thing I got. Ooh, how cute. I look cute. Let me snap some pics for Insta'.

AUGUSTUS: Right. Do we need to know what your face looks like? *Again?* Give me something. Give me some substance. Do we need to know what your face looks like one more time? The ape playing Narcissus. Because there's a lot beyond that. Don't fall in. It's not that interesting, after all. I know your face is beautiful. Everybody's face is beautiful. That's okay. But I know you have a lot going on in that heart space. Let me see. Let us see. What's in the heart space? I know it's going to be shaky. It's like the bird trying to leave the nest. Legs are sticks. The legs don't know what they are doing in the beginning. The wings don't really work, but it's okay. You're not there already. If you think you're there already, you're not there. That's the thing. And I'm not saying *I'm* there. I'm just saying, if you think you're there already, you're not there. If you think you have it all figured out, look again.

EBEN: That's the core precept in Yoga, isn't it? You come back to this mind-blowing understanding that I know that I know nothing.

AUGUSTUS: That's from Socrates. And Yoga. Yes. Socrates was a Yogi in his own right, in my opinion.

EBEN: Because then you're not caught up in thinking you know everything. Thinking things are supposed to be a certain way because *you know*. What an egocentric way of going about the world. I know this, therefore if it's not that it's all wrong. The Universe is ineffably vast. You think you know as much as the Universe?

AUGUSTUS: Good luck with that idea. Let me know what the Universe says.

EBEN: You have all the answers? Okay. Let's see. Get out of the mind and into the heart. *Get out of the mind and into the heart.*

AUGUSTUS: That's such a beautiful one. That's a shirt. We're doing that on a t-shirt.

EBEN: Out of the mind. Into the heart. The heart is connected to the universal intelligence. The one, the source of all things.

AUGUSTUS: It is interesting that when you feel emotions your heart responds, your brain doesn't respond. I mean your brain responds but your heart is really the reaction you feel. Your heart's the one that responds. It beats and senses vibrations. It is the sunlit key to living and being.

EBEN: How did humanity get this caught up in the mind? Because we see out of eyes that are at the top of our body?

AUGUSTUS: For one—and it's a big one—it's this material culture. This canned goods culture that we've created. We're just caught in the mind and we've become over physicalized. We've become over materialized. It's a tragedy of industrialization. It's a tragedy of capitalism. There's an inherent double-edged sword. Like our great grandfather or uncle, whoever he is to us exactly, Jack Parsons. He said the double-edged sword of this whole thing.

EBEN: He said 'freedom is a two-edged sword'.

AUGUSTUS: Freedom is a two-edged sword, baby. That's it.

EBEN: You have to tap in with the truth. If you're reliant on a government to perpetuate your freedom then you're in for a really scary realization.

AUGUSTUS: If you're solely identified with your mind, which has billions of different reception areas, little dudes in tanks, pushing buttons up there, little green women walking around pulling levers. That can get messy. The heart to me is the sun. It's the solar plexus. It's where the truth is. I'm not discounting the mind. The mind is a beautiful slave, but a terrible master.

EBEN: You hit it on the head though, you're right, it is a tragedy of industrialization. It seems to me that communism is a trap of not living. Communism is an intellectual trap, because you think, 'oh, that's really good, everyone's going to have all the same stuff, but someone at the top is in charge of controlling all of it'.

AUGUSTUS: Do you bring up Communism because you feel like that's where we're going?

EBEN: I don't know. It's a dance we seem to come back to all the time in our culture, living an industrialized or capitalistic life. As in, is Communism a better idea? Or Socialism? And it seems like the liberal ethos is really pushing a state of singularity of humanity. They feel more comfortable 'living' if everyone talks the same, thinks the same, looks the same. And that is a universally false paradigm. It's not a reality that any of us can live in. I was at the beach the other day and I was flung out to Venus. I'd taken this puff of weed, eaten mushrooms. Looked around walking up and down the beach. I start doing this breathing in and then humming. Humming is really powerful to clear the mind.

AUGUSTUS: Yes. Humming is born out of bees and the OM. It's the divine bee energy. Bees are all that.

EBEN: Yes. And all of a sudden I'm looking around at the beach and I'm going, 'Oh my God, it's all an illusion'.

AUGUSTUS: In a good way?

EBEN: Neither good nor bad. You know the story of The Tower of Babel? Basically, humanity—all the people on the planet—were building this tower to God. God got angry about it, destroyed the tower and split up all the people. They went into various tribes and God gave them all different languages. They couldn't communicate and work together. And I'm looking around at all of it on the beach—the skinny people, fit people, fat people, different skin colors, dark, white, darker, whiter, darker. We're all one thing. But we've been broken up into these lives of identification. So most people don't know where to turn, except for into the illusion and the drama. It's all a trap. It's all a trap because we're all the same animal.

AUGUSTUS: My belief is that the only way we get out of the trap is meditation. Because meditation is the only way I've experienced how we get to that source. How we get to the understanding of similarity of spirit and heart. Elysium, Atlantis, Utopia, Eden, whatever you want to call it, that world is a world grounded in meditation. Meditation is the pathway because we *can't* talk it out. That's the whole Babel game. The different voices won't get us to God or true life. We need to *not* speak. And where do we do that? Meditation. In the heart space. In meditation we can finally hear. In meditation we get to feel the true sound, which is silence. There is no argument with silence.

EBEN: We are one being, we are all a multitude of manifestations of the same thing. Equality in the Babel paradigm is not real equality. In the heart paradigm equality is real. There is no intellectual equality but there *is* intuitive equality. The mind is intellectual. The heart is intuitive.

AUGUSTUS: Otherwise you're dying for false lives. I just heard Ram Dass say he was sitting with his mother when she was dying. He said she was under the influence of morphine. He said was under the influence of mescaline. One night they were super high and started having a conversation that they had never had before. Very intimate. True. Honest. The veils gone. It was days before she died. They woke up in the morning and his mother was upset, she said they shouldn't have had that conversation, that she was drugged. Ram Dass laughed because that was the truest conversation he had ever had with his mother! I bring this up because I feel like it goes along with the illusion statement, because she was fixed in her illusion. She couldn't even live outside of her paradigm. She's dying for a manufactured life that's not even real. But I guess it was real to her. So who am I to say? I guess she gets another round on the wheel.

EBEN: Being thick in identity is causing more chaos and separation. The people with power benefit from people being divided. This needs to change, obviously. They benefit off of us fighting against each other. Trying to convince each other that they're wrong and we're right. Do you walk out into nature and all the trees are the same? All the leaves look the same? All the flowers are the same color and have the same smell? No, the variety is part of the oneness. On your hand; do you have five pinkies? I don't, it wouldn't make sense. You have a thumb and an index and a middle and a ring and a pinky for a reason.

AUGUSTUS: And then they create the whole.

EBEN: With humanity all of the differences create the whole. If you're living the life that someone else is telling you to live or else you're not doing a good job, your life will be filled with discontent and unfulfillment. If you live from the heart and you find yourself penniless, I guarantee you'll be happier than with a billion dollars in the bank and living someone else's life. To me, that's a life worth dying for—living from the heart. A life lived from the heart space. That's a life worth dying for. Time's running out.

AUGUSTUS: Well, when you start truly living time isn't real anyway.

EBEN: But I'm saying time is running out with the spirit. Spirit doesn't have the patience for us to continue down the path of not living from the truth. The future will be very unkind to the unconscious.

AUGUSTUS: Spirit has the patience, but it's going to show you what it needs to show you.

EBEN: Exactly. It'll wipe it all out. It'll wipe it clean. The Universe will say, 'hey, okay, cool, you want to be unconscious and not live in your truth? All right. We'll wipe the whole thing clean. Start over'.

AUGUSTUS: Start asking the uncomfortable questions.

EBEN: We think going to Mars will solve it? Nope.

AUGUSTUS: Start asking those questions your heart always wanted you to ask.

EBEN: I saw this quote from Louise hay and Byron Katie. They said, when you get quiet, ask yourself, *'is it true?'*

AUGUSTUS: Beautiful. That lets your higher Self in.

EBEN: Do I need the BMW? Is it true? *I need the BMW. I need the BMW. I need the BMW.* Are you sure you need that to live from the heart? It's interesting even doing that exercise just now. I can feel the false vibration in my body. When I say I need the BMW it feels empty. And I *had* the BMW! The most expensive one money could buy. I was miserable.

AUGUSTUS: That BMW's in a graveyard somewhere.

EBEN: There's no resonance when I'm saying that I need the BMW. But then all of a sudden, I say, 'I need to live from the heart'. And there's this warmth. *I live from the heart. I live from the heart. I live from the heart.* It emanates from the center of my being. I feel it in my hands.

AUGUSTUS: That's music. That's mantra. Careful what music you're letting in. Careful what mantra you're letting in. Careful what sound you're letting in. Listen to those voices that are high vibrations, high frequencies. They love you. They want your heart to be well. They love your heart. Get conscious.

EBEN: We're just here to say 'get conscious'. Get into the moment. Start living from the moment and then that'll reveal everything you need.

AUGUSTUS: And it's not frantic. Living in the moment. It's not a frantic goal you live in. Just drop in. Slowly. A flower in the air. Drop into meditation. Get silent. Then move from there. Let there be a beautiful lotus. A jasmine fragranced springboard.

EBEN: I love that. I think that's it then. How can you live deeper in the moment today? Just for today. Not tomorrow. Not yesterday. Just today. Are you living a life worth dying for today? An honest life. What is a life worth dying for? That's a meditation. Love everybody, particularly yourself.

Eben Britton and Augustus Britton are brothers.
They grew up in New York City and Los
Angeles. Eben is host of The Eben Flow podcast.
Augustus is a journalist and novelist. They are
both Yogis. They are both people. They are both
here. Now. They collaborate frequently.

For more information:
contact@ebenbritton.com

+ Peace & Love & Truth +

had ye but faith ye could move mountains